Hindi Lang

For Kids /

Beginners

Speak Hindi Instantly

By

Shalu Sharma

GW00858895

Table of contents

Introduction

Teaching Hindi to children living in foreign countries is a hard thing to do. Every time I visit my relatives in England and to the American continent (USA and Canada), I find their children speaking back in English. They seem to understand Hindi all right but they are not able to respond back in Hindi. It's not bad parenting; it's just that they live in countries where Hindi is not spoken and most of the time they are surrounded by children who speak English. In countries where children have to learn swimming, play soccer or chess, go to music lessons and so on; this gives them little time to learn the Hindi language. In spite of all these essential activities, most Indian parents make sure that their children take part in cultural programmes and activities. However no matter how hard they try, some children are still not able to learn Hindi no matter what they do.

Parents living abroad should definitely be teaching the Hindi language to their children otherwise they are missing out on their cultural heritage. One linking factor between parents and their children living in foreign countries is the Hindi language. It's like a bridge for them, their children and India. I have heard many non-resident Indian parents regret that they did not try hard enough to teach the language to their children. Communication in the same language is the link between them and India hence it is vital that children are able to at least understand some Hindi.

I am not saying English is a bad thing; most people in India learn the English language which is one of the most important international languages of the world. But Hindi is something that links people living in the west back to India.

What is this book about?

This book is all about teaching children basic worlds, phrases and some conversational Hindi to get them started. The book will start off with the Hindi alphabets. Although parents here may not wish to teach them the alphabets but nonetheless, I have included them in the first chapter as a book on Hindi would not be complete without a chapter on the alphabets and its pronunciation. I have not included the "Devanagri" script after the first chapter to make things easier as learning alphabets in the Devanagir script is a completely different ball game together.

The book then goes through some of the most common words, phrases and sentences a child will encounter. These are the ones they will use the most with their parents such as food and drinks words, colours, food, Hindi around the house hold, words they are likely to use in the garden and so. These are then accompanied by phrases and then sentences. Most of these words, phrases and sentences are the ones they are most likely to use in day to day life with parents, visitors and at social gatherings. Hopefully learning them would allow them to converse in Hindi at home with parents, parent's friends, grandparents and on social occasions.

Who is this book for?

The book is not aimed at any particular age group. The book can be used by anyone and for any purpose. The book can also be used by children of non-Indian origin or even by those who simply want to learn some Hindi.

This book will be useful to Indian children living in foreign countries, travellers visiting India, those wishing to learn Hindi, foreigners married to Indians, or beginners of the Hindi language.

How to use this book?

Don't let yourself be discouraged by the complex grammar, script and the pronunciation of Hindi. This book contains Hindi words, phrases and sentences that will be useful in everyday use which means that the user will be able to learn, memorise, utilise and speak basic Hindi instantly without learning any of the grammar or script.

The best way to use this book is to repeat the words several times in order to memorise them.

For example, if you want to say,

"*My name is Neal*" in Hindi then this would translate to "*Mera naam Neal hai*". So the best way to learn this is to memorise the phrase "*Mera naam Neal hai*" several times.

I believe this is the easiest and the quickest method to learn the language. Repeat the words, phrases and sentences till it becomes natural so you do not need to think about what you are saying.

The book is written in English hence children and beginners would have no issues learning these words, phrases and sentence. English translation is written side-by-side and exactly the way it should be pronounced. Many words and phrases have been deliberately repeated in some chapters. I have included some conversational Hindi which a child or a beginner might encounter.

One of the key distinctive features of Hindi is the "nasal" sounds for example as in 'bon voyage', 'uncle' and 'honk' - just like the sound coming from the letter "n". Please note that I have written the words in the way it should be pronounced phonetically. I have not taken the nasal sounds very much in consideration. This is because some sections of Indian society particularly those who are not native Hindi speakers are not able to produce the nasal sounds. But they do speak Hindi and get by perfectly alright. Therefore this book is for those who wish to learn quickly without worrying about semantics. In addition, no complex grammar has been used just to make things easier.

Hindi vowels and consonants

The Hindi language is written in the Devanagri script.

Hindi consists of 36 consonants, traditionally 11 vowels (some say 13). Here are the 12 most commonly used Hindi vowels.

Hindi vowels

अ - आ - इ - ई - उ - ऊ - ए - ऐ - ओ - औ - अं - अः

a   aa   e   ee   u   oo   aay   o   au   um   am   aha

The vowels come in pairs with one exception

(a) as in about

(aa) as in barn

(e) as in miss

(ee) as in deep

(u) as in put

(oo) as in soon

(aay) as in make

(o) as in rode

(au) as in out

(um) – as in umbrella

(aha) - as in ahead

Hindi Consonants

क - ख - ग - घ - ङ - च - छ - ज - झ - ञ - ट - ठ - ड - ढ - ण
k - kh - g - gh -n - ch-chh- j - jh - n - t - th - d - dh - n

त - थ - द - ध - न - प - फ - ब - भ - म - य - र - ल - व - श
t - th - d - dh -n - p - ph - b -bh -m - y - r- l - v -sh

ष - स - ह   क्ष - त्र - ज्ञ
sh -s - h   ksh - tr - gya

(k) as in Cat

(kh) as in Khaki

(g) as in Grass

(gh) as in Ghana

(n) as in Namibia

(ch) as in chuck

(chh) as in Chat

(j) as in Jam

(jh) as in Jakarta

(n) as in Nigeria

(t) as in Tamara

(th) as in Thack

(d) as in dog

(dh) as in Dah

(n) as in "na"

(t) as in Tap

(th) as in Thumb

(d) as in Dumb

(dh) sound like "dha"

(n) as in Noh

(p) as in Pam

(ph) sounds like "pha"

(b) as in bum

(bh) sound like "bha" as in Bhaji

(m) as in mum

(y) sound like "ye" as in Yes

(r) sounds like "ra"

(l) as in Love

(v or w) as in work

(sh) as in sham

(sh) sound like "ss"

(s) sounds like "so"

(h) sound like "ha"

(ksh) sounds like "chha"

(tr) sounds like "thra"

(gya) as in gyan

Most commonly used Hindi word and phrases

Hello - Namaste or Pranam

Thank you – Dhanyevaad or Shukriya

Please – Kripya

Excuse me or Pardon me – Chama karay (or maaj kijiye)

Listen - Suneye

You – Aap (older than you); Tum (smaller than you)

What is your name – Tumhara kya naam hai

My name is Krishna – Mera naam Krishna hai

What – Kya

When – Kab

Why – Ku

Who – Kaun

Where - Kaha

Which – Kaun sa

Good luck – Subh kamnaye

Shop – Dukaan

Let's go – Chalo

See you later – Phir milengay

Okay – Thik hai

Yes – Haa

No – Nahi

Like – Pasand

Left - Baye

Right – Daaye

Good – Accha

Bad – Kharab

Clothes – Kapra

Shirt – Kameez

Give – Lo

Take – Do

Small – Chota

Big - Small

Same – Ek jaisa

Different – Alag

Broken – Tuta

Help - Madaad

It's broken – Tut gaya

This – Yeh

Today – Aaj

Tomorrow – Kal

And – Aur

Go – Jao

Student - Vidyarthi

Wedding (marriage) - Shaadi

Day after tomorrow – Parso

Day before yesterday – Parso (same as day after tomorrow)

I don't know – Mujhay nahi malum

I know – Mujhay malum hai

Very good – Bahut achha

Birthday – Janam din

Happy birthday – Janam din ki subh kamnaye

Many happy returns of the day- Din ki bahut subh kamnaye

Today is my birthday – Aaj mera janam din hai

I must go – Mujhay jaana hai

Where are you – Tum kaha ho

I am here – Mai yaha hu

May I have tea – Kya Mujhay chai mil sakti hai

Who are you – Tum kaun ho

I need to go to a party – Mujhay party mei jana hai

When will you come – Tum kun aawoge

I'm coming – Mai aa raha hu (boy); Mai aa rahi ho (girl)

Let eat – Chalo khate hai

Take me to the hospital – Mujhay hospital le chalo

I am a doctor – Mai doctor hu

I am a student – Mai vidyarthi hu

Do you speak English – Kya aap English bolte hai (to boy); Kya aap English bolti hai (to girl)

Do you speak Hindi – Kya aap Hindi bolte hai (to boy); Kya aap Hindi bolti hai (to girl)

Time and duration in Hindi

Morning – Subah

Night – Raat

Evening – Sham

Afternoon – Do pehar

Now – Abhi

Before - Pahlay

Later – Baad may

Not now – Abhi nahi

Its night – Raat ho gaya

Its morning – Subah ho gaya

In the night – Raat mai

In the morning – Subhah mai

When are we going – Kub jana hai

Let's go now – Abhi chalo

We will go later – Baad mei chalengay

One O' clock – Ek bajay

Two O' clock – Do bajay

Yesterday – Kal

Hour – Ghanta

1 hour – Ek ghanta

2 hours – Do ghanta

Day – Din

Week – Hafta

Month – Maheena

Year – Saal

Watch – Ghari

What is the time – Samay kya huwa hai

It's one O' clock – Abhi ek baja hai

Shall we go now – Kya abhi chal saktay hai

We will go later – Baad mei challenge

I must go – Mujhay jaana hai

I am going – Mai ha raha hu (boy); Mai jaa rahi hu (girl)

How long will it take – Kitna der lagega

It will take 1 hour – Ek ghanta lagega

Can you come now – Kya abhi aa saktay ho (to boy); Kya abhi aa sakti ho (to girl)

Hindi when meeting and greeting

Hello - Namaste or Pranam

Bye – Alvida

Uncle – Chacha

Aunty – Chachi

House – Ghar

Inside – Andar

Welcome – Swagatam, Swagat

Car- Gaari

Cold - Thanda

Hot – Garam

Weather – Mausam

Mine – Mayra

Yours – Tumhara

Kiska – Who's

Ours – Hamara

Come inside – Andar aayiye

Thank you - Dhanyevaad

Hello uncle – Namaste uncle or Namaste chacha ji

Hello aunty – Namaste aunty or Namaste chachi ji

Hello son – Namaste beta

How's the weather – Mausam kaisa hai

Nice too meet you - Aap se milkay khusee hui

Is it cold today – Kya aaj thanda hai

Is it hot today – Kya aaj garam hai

You are welcome – Aap ka swagat hai

How are you - App kaisay hai

Please come in – Aap andar aaiye

I am fine (boy) – Mai accha hu

I am fine (girl) – Mai acchi hu

Please give me your coat – Aap apna coat Mujhay deejiye

How old are you – Mai 10 saal ka hu

This is for your – Yeh aap ke liye hai

What is your name – Tumhara naam kya hai

My name is Amit – Mera naam Amit hai

Where do you live – Aap kaha rahtay hai

What would you like to drink – Aap kya pee-jeeyega

Thanda ya garam – Cold or hot

Please sit down – Kripya baitiye

You look nice – Aap acchay lag rahay hai

Hindi when saying goodbye

Goodbye – Namaste or alvida

Bye uncle – Namaste uncle or alvida uncle

Bye aunty – Namaste aunty or alvida aunty

See you later – Phir milayenge

Please come again – Phir aayiyega

I must go – Mai chalta hu (male); Mai chalti hu (girl)

Where is your car – Aap ki gaari kaha hai

Where did you park the car – Apne gaari kaha park kiya

When will you meet again – Aap phir kab milengay

When will we meet again – Hum log phir kab milengay

Are you going – Kya aap jaa rahay hai

This is your coat – Ye aap ka coat hai

I will see you to the door (boy saying) – Mai aap ko darwaza tak chhor aata hi (boy)

I will see you to the door (girl saying) – Mai aap ko darwaza tak chhor aati hi (girl)

When – Kab

Where – Kaha

Let's go – Chalo

Hindi numbers

One – Ek

Two – Do

Three –Theen

Four - Char

Five - Panch

Six - Cchay

Seven – Sath

Eight - Aath

Nine - Nau

Ten - Dus

Eleven – Ekgyarah

Twelve - Barah

Thirteen – Therah

Fourteen - Chaudah

Fifteen - Pandrah

Sixteen - Solah

Seventeen - Satarah

Eighteen - Aatarah

Nineteen - Unnees

Twenty – Bees

Thirty - Tees

Forty - Chalis

Fifty – Pachas

Sixty – Saath

Seventy – Sattar

Eighty – Assi

Ninety – Nabbay

Hundred – Sau

Thousand – Hazar

Ten thousand – Dus Hazar

Hundred thousand – Ek Lakh

One million - Dus Lakh

Ten million – Ek Crore

Names of common Indian sweets

Gajar Halwa - Halva made of carrots

Gulab Jamun – Round syrupy sweet balls

Rasgulla – Ball syrupy dessert

Jalebi – Orange spring like sweets

Ras Malai – Made of homemade juicy cheese dessert

Kheer – Rice pudding

Kulfi – Indian ice cream

Laddu – Ball shaped sweets

Lassi – Yogurt drink

Pedra – Dry flat sweets made of milk

I want a gulab jamun- Muhe ek gulab jamun chaiye

I want kulfi – Mujhay kulfi do

I want to eat rice pudding – Mujhay kheer khana ka mun hai

Colours in Hindi

Red - Laal

Purple - Baigni

Gold - Sunahra

Silver - Chandi

Green - Hara

Yellow - Peela

White - Safaid or Ujlaa

Black - Kala

Brown - Bhura

Orange – Narangi

Blue – Neela

Pink - Gulabi

This is red – Ye laal hai

This is yellow – Ye peela hai

This toy is red – Ye khelona (toy) red hai

The red house – Laal makaan (or ghar)

This red sari – Ye laal sari

This green shirt – Ye hara shirt

I like brown – Mujhay bhura pasand hai

Give me the green one – Mujhay green wala dejiye

I don't like the red one – Mujhay laal wala acha nahi laga

Common food and drinks in Hindi

Tea – Chai

Water – Paani

Juice – Russ

Fruits – Phal

Rice – Chawal

Lentils – Daal

Chapatti – Roti

Bread – Paow roti

Butter - Makhan

Fish – Machli

Eggs - Aanda

Cheese – Paneer

Spices – Masala

Milk – Dhudh

Salt – Namak

Sugar – Cheeni

Chilli – Mirch

Coriander –Dhaniya

Turmeric – Haldi

Rice pudding – Kheer

Mithai – Indian sweets

Kofta – Meat balls

Corn – Makai

Radish – Mooli

Peanuts – Moom fali

Chicken – Murgi

Lemon – Nimboo

Onions – Pyaj

Mint – Pudeena

Kidney beans – Rajma

Tomato – Tamatar

Sultanas – Kiss miss

Peas – Matar

I want tea – Mujhay chai chaiye

I want water - Mujhay paani chaiye

Can I have a glass of water - Kya Mujhay ek glass paani milega

Can I have something to drink – Kya Mujhay peenay ke liye kutch milega

May I have coke – Kya muhe coke milega

May I have orange juice – Kya muhe narangi ka russ (or orange juice) milega

I am hungry – Mujhay bhuk lagi hai (girl); Muhe bhuk laga hai (boy)

I am very hungry – Mujhay bahut bhuk lagi hai

I am not hungry – Mujhay bhuk nahi hai

Let's eat – Chalo khatay hai

Let's go to MacDonald's - MacDonald's chaltay hai

Are you hungry – Kya tumhay bhuk lagi hai

Eating words and phrases

Food – Khana

Drink – Peena

Breakfast – Subhah ka kahna (or nasta)

Lunch – Din ka khana

Dinner – Raat ka khana

Table – Maiz

Kitchen – Rasoi ghar

Vegetarian – Shakahari

Meat eater – Mansahari

Vegetable – Subje

Meat – Ghost (or maans)

Beef – Gai ka maans

Pork – Suwar ka maans

Fish – Machli

Fork and knife – Kata aur churi

Spoon – Khamach

To eat – Khao

To drink - Peeyo

Eat vegetable – Subje khao

Meat khao – Ghost khao

I am hungry – Mujhay bhuk lagi hai

I am not hungry - Mujhay bhuk nahi nahi hai

Give me food – Mijhe khana do

Cook food – Khana banao

I want to eat vegetables – Mujhay subje khana hai

I want to eat meat – Mujhay (meat) maans khana hai

I want to eat fish – Mujhay machli khana hai

Can you cook chicken – Kya aap chicken bana saktay hai

Can you cook curry – Kya aap curry bana saktay hai

I want lunch – Mujhay lunch (dopahar ka khana) chaiye

I want dinner – Mujhay dinner (raat ka khana) chaiye

This food is good – Ye khana acha hai

This food is bad – Ye khana kharab hai

Sweet – Meetha

Sour - Khata

Hot – Garam

Cold - Thanda

This is hot – Ye garam hai

This is cold – Ye thanda hai

This food is hot – Ye khana hot hai

This food is cold – Ye kahana cold hai

Can you warm the food – Khana garam kar dijiye

Spicy - Masaledar

This is spicy – Ye (masaledar) spicy hai

Stomach - Pait

My stomach is hurting – Mera pait dard kar raha hai

Would you like to eat something - Kya aap kutch kahan pasand karenge

I am going to the restaurant – Mai restaurant jai raha hu (boy); Mai restaurant ja rahi hu (girl)

What do you want to eat – Kya khaogay

What do you want to drink – Kya peeogay

Relation words

Boy - Ladka

Girl - Ladki

Son - beta

Daughter- Beti

Mother- Maa, Mata, Mata ji, Mummy

Father – Papa, Pita, Pita ji, Bapu

Husband - Pati

Wife - Patni (also biwi)

Man - Aadmi (also mard)

Woman - Aurat

Child – Bachha

Older brother – Bhaiya (also bara bhai)

Younger brother – Anuj (also Chota bhai)

Sister - Bahen

Older sister - Bari bahen

Younger sister - Choti bahen

Uncle – Chacha (Chacha ji for respect)

Aunty – Chahi (Chachi ji for respect)

Mother's brother – Mama (Mama ji for respect). Remember 'Mama Shri' for Shakuni in Mahabharata.

Mother's sister – Mausi (Mausi ji for respect)

Father's sister - Phuaa

Mum's father – Nana ji

Mum's mother – Nani ji

Father's mother – Dadi ji

Father's father – Dada ji

Friend – Dhost (or mitr)

Brother's wife – Bhabhi ji

Grandson – Pota

Granddaughter - Poti

Mother in law – Saas

Father in law – Sasur

Son in law – Damaad

Daughter in law – Bahu

Sister's husband – Bahnoi

Neighbour - Parosi

Female friend to another female – Saheli

Buddy – Yaar

Companion – Saathi

Teacher – Guru

Student – Chhatra (or vidyarthi)

Education related words and phrases in Hindi

Work – Kaam

School - Paatshala

Do work - Kaam karo

Do your homework – Apna homework karo

Education – Shiksha (Padhai)

Reading (to read) – Padha

Writing (to write) – Likhna

Book - Kitab

Reading a book – Kitab padhana

Pen - Kalam

Common do some work - Chalo padhai karo

Maths – Ganit

Sums - Hesaab

Biology – Jeev vigyaan

Do Maths – Hisaan (or ganit) karo

I am reading a book – Mai ek kitab padh raha hu (boy); Mai ek kitab padh rahi hu (girl)

I am writing – Mai likh raha hu (boy); Mai likh rahi hu (girl)

I am going to school – Mai school jaa raha hu (boy); Mai school jaa rahi hi (girl)

How far is the school – School (paatshala) kita dur hai

Household words, phrases and sentences

House – Ghar

Room – Kumra

Wall – Deewar

Roof – Chhath

Stairs - Sidhee

Key – Chabhi

Lock - Thaala

Bathroom – Latrine

Window – khidki

Door – Darwaza

Cot – Khatiya

Cupboard – Almeera

Plants - Paudhey

Iron - Isteree

Bed - Palang

Pillow – Takeeya

Blanket – Kambal

Bin - Kura daan

Mirror – Aayina, Shesha

Light – Roshni

Electricity – Bizli

Lamp - Deepak

Tap - Nal

Chair – Kursee

Candle - Mombatti

Carpet – Kaleen

Clothes – Kapra

Pen – Kalam

Needle – Sui

Thread – Dhagaa

Knife – Churee

Oil – Theel

Ring - Anguthee

Gold – Sona

Silver – Chandi

Bucket – Balti

Umbrella – Chaata

Basket – Tokree

Cup – Pyala

Box - Sandook

Lid - Dhakan

To buy – Khareedna

To shower – Nahana

I want to take a shower – Mujhay nahana hai

I need a pen - Mujhay ek pen chaiye

I need to buy clothes – Mujhay kapra khareedna hai

This is mine – Ye mara hai

This is yours – Ye tumhara

Who's is this – Ye kiska hai

I want to go home – Mujhay ghar jaana hai

Vegetables in Hindi

Ginger – Adrakh

Garlic – Lahsun

Tomato – Tamatar

Onion - Pyaj

Cucumber – Kakri, Kheera

Chilli – Mirch

Red chilli – Lal mirch

Green chilli – Hari mirch

Cabbage – Patha gobi

Coriander - Dhaniya

Drumstick – Sahjan

Eggplant – Baigan

Mint leaf - Pundina

Cauliflower – Phul gobi

Carrot – Gajar

Corn – Makai

Potato – Aalo

Sweet potato – Sakarkand

Radish – Mooli

Pumpkin – Kaddu

Peas – Matar

Ladies finger – Okra, Bhindi

Animals and birds in Hindi

Animal – Janwar

Wild – Junglee

Tame – Paltu

Zoo – Cheriya khana

Bear – Bhalu

Crocodile – Magarmach

Donkey – Gadha

Fox - Lomri

Dog – Kutta

Cat – Billi

Elephant - Haathi

Mouse – Chuha

Rabbit – Khargosh

Frog - Medhak

Camel – Oonth

Sheep – Bher

Jackal – Seeyar

Rhinoceros - Genda

Goat – Bakri

Pig - Suwar

Lion – Sher

Tiger – Bagh

Squirrel – Gilahri

Fish – Machli

Spider - Makri

Horse – Ghora

Cow – Gai

Turtle - Kachua

Monkey – Bandar

Wolf – Lomri

Snake - Saanp

This is a dog - Ye dog hai

This is a cat - Ye cat hai

This is a wild cat – Ye jungle billi hai

Let's go to the zoo - Cheriya khana chalte hai

Nature words in Hindi

Nature – Prakriti

Planet Earth – Prithvi

Wind – Hawa

Cloud – Badal

Lightning – Bizli

Rainbow – Indra-dhanush

Rain – Paani barasna

Sky – Aasman

Moon – Chand

Sun – Surya, Suraj

Star – Taara

River – Nadhi

Soil – Mitti

Dust – Dhul

Mountain – Pahar

Storm – Tufan

Sunshine – Dhoop

Sea – Samundra, sagar

Ocean – Mahasagar (maha meaning great)

River – Nadi

Rock – Patthar

Snow – Barf

Volcano – Jwalamukhi

Space – Antariksh

Environment - Vatavaran

Sand – Baloo, Reth

Pond – Talaab

Lake – Jheel

Grass – Ghas

Flower – Phool

Plant – Paudha

Forest – Jungle

Human organs in Hindi

Body – Shareer

Bone - Haddi

Human – Insaan, Manav

Head – Sir

Face – Chehra, Muh

Forehead – Matha

Eyebrow - Bhau, Palak

Moustache – Muchay

Lip – Hointh

Teeth – Danth

Beard - Dhadhi

Skin – Khaal, Chamri, Twacha

Nose – Naal

Ear – Kaan

Teeth - Danth

Mouth – Muh

Tongue – Jeeb

Cheek – Gaal

Eye - Aankh

Hair – Baal

Head – Sar

Shoulder – Kandha

Chest - Chathi

Neck – Gardan

Throat - Gala

Stomach - Pait

Arm – Bah

Palm of the hand - Hatheli

Hand – Haath

Armpit - Kankh

Fingers – Ungli

Wrist - Kalai

Thumb - Angutha

Elbow - Kohani

Fist - Muthee

Nail - Nakhun

Knee – Ghutna

Leg –Tang

Thigh - Jangh

Foot - Pare

This is my hand – Ye mera hand hai

This is my leg – Ye mera tang hai

My stomach hurts – Mera pait dard kar raha hai

My neck hurts – Mera gardan dard kar raha hai

Common fruits in Hindi

Apple - Saib

Banana - Kela

Grapes - Angoor

Groundnut – Moomfali

Mango – Aam

Papaya – Papeeta

Watermelon – Tarbooza

Pomegranate – Aanaar

Orange – Santara, Narangi

Jackfruit – Kathahul

Guava – Amroodh

Coconut – Narial

Dates – Khajoor

Pear – Naspathi

Conversations

Conversation with a guest from the moment they come in

Conversation when someone comes to the house from the moment you open the door. How to greet someone from opening the door onwards?

(You) Hello – Namaste

(Guest) Namaste

(You) Please come in – Andar aa-e-yay

(Guest) Thank you – Dhanyevaad

(You) How are you – Aap kaise hai

(Guest) I am fine, how are you – Mai thik hu, tum kaisay ho

(You) I am also fine – Mai bhi achha hu (boy); Mai bhi acchi hu (girl)

(You) Please sit down – App baitiye

(Guest) Dhanyevaad

(You) What will you drink – Aap kya piyengay

(Guest) I will drink tea – Mai chai piyunga (boy); Mai chai piyungi (girl)

(You) I will make the tea – Mai chai banata hu (boy); Mai chai banati hu (girl)

(You) Do you take sugar and milk - Kya aap dudh aur cheeni laytay hai

(You) Here's the tea – Ye chai lejiye

(Guest) Thank you – Danyevaad

(Guest) Tea is nice – Chai acchi hai

Conversation between dad and child about studies

(Dad) What did you study today - Tumnay aaj kya padhai kiya

(Child) Nothing – Kutch nahi

(Dad) Why not – Kyu nahi

(Dad) Come on take your English book out - Chalo English ki kitab nikalo

(Child) No I don't want to study – Mujhay padhnay ka man nahi hai

(Dad) Why not – Ku nahi

(Child) I want to play computer games – Mujhay computer games khelna hai

(Dad) No, you can't play any more – Nahi, tum ab nahi khel saktay

(Child) Okay – Thik hai

(Dad) Did you do your homework – Kya tumnay homework kiya

(Child) No, I did not – Nahi mainay nahi kiya

(Dad) Come on do your homework – Chalo apna homework karo

(Dad) What kind of homework do you have - Kaisa homework mila hai

(Child) I have maths today – Aaj maths mila hai

(Dad) Okay show it to me –Thik hai chalo Mujhay dikhao

Child saying I am not well

(Child) I am not well – Mera tabiyath nahi tikh hai

(Dad or mum) - What is the problem – Problem kya hai

(Child) I have stomach upset – Mera pait dard kar raha hai

(Child) I have a fever – Mujhay fever hai

(Dad or mum) Let me take a look – Mujhay dekhay do

(Dad or mum) – Yes, you have a fever – Haa, tumhay fever hai

(Dad or mum) – You go to bed, I will call a doctor – Yum bed mai jayo, mai doctor ko call karta hu (or karti hu – for mum)

Child) Okay – Thik hai

Conversation between child and mother for dinner

(Mum) Come and eat your food – Aao aa-kay khana khao

(Child) Not now, I am playing – Abhi nahi, mai khel raha hu (boy); Abhi nahi, mai khel rahi hu

(Mum) Come now – Abhi aao

(Child) Give me five minutes – Panch minute dijiye

(Mum) Okay – Thik hai

(Child) What have you made – Aap ne kya banaya hai

(Mum) Rice and chicken curry – Chawal aur chicken curry

(Child) I like it – Mujhay pasand hai

(Mum) OK come quick – Thik hai jaldi aao

(Child) I am coming – Mai mai aa raha hu (boy); Mai aa rahi hu (girl)

(Mum) I am waiting – Mai tumhara intazaar kar rahi hu

Message from the author

Thank you for buying this book. I hope it will be useful to children and to those starting out on learning the Hindi language. Hindi can be a confusing language but do not be discouraged, it can be learnt. My suggestion is to watch lots of Hindi movies and listen to Hindi music. Also make sure that you lean the words, phrases and sentences given in this book by heart as they are most commonly used words and phrases in the Hindi language. Also when you have memorised many of them, then this will give you the confidence to take the next step in learning Hindi.

You can listen to me speak some of the Hindi words, phrases and sentences here http://www.shalusharma.com/hindi-phrases. If you get stuck on any of the words or phrases or wanted me to pronounce then feel free to get in touch from my website http://www.shalusharma.com/contact or simply email me on bihar123@gmail.com. If required, I can record them for you and send them as an mp3 file. Please do not hesitate if you need help in learning the Hindi language.

Here are my other books:

Hinduism For Kids: Beliefs And Practices - ISBN-10: 1495370429
Essential Hindi Words And Phrases For Travelers To India - ISBN-10: 1492752517
India For Kids: Amazing Facts About India - ISBN-10: 149470997X
Life and Works of Aryabhata - ISBN-10: 1495351386
Mahatma Gandhi For Kids And Beginners - ASIN: B00ICABNHO
India Travel Survival Guide For Women - ISBN-10:

149122648X
Essential India Travel Guide: Travel Tips And Practical
Information - ISBN-10: 1497391679

Printed in Great Britain
by Amazon.co.uk, Ltd.,
Marston Gate.